Georgia

BY MARGARET LAWLER

CONTENT CONSULTANT
George W. Justice, PhD
Senior Lecturer
Department of History, Anthropology, and Philosophy
University of North Georgia

Core Library

An Imprint of Abdo Publishing
abdobooks.com

abdobooks.com

Published by Abdo Publishing, a division of ABDO, PO Box 398166, Minneapolis, Minnesota 55439.

Printed in the United States of America, North Mankato, Minnesota.
052022
092022

Cover Photo: Shutterstock Images
Interior Photos: Andrew Brunk/Shutterstock Images, 4–5; Red Line Editorial, 6 (Georgia), 6 (USA); ESB Professional/Shutterstock Images, 9; Rod Clement Photography/Shutterstock Images, 12–13, 43; Everett Collection/Shutterstock Images, 15; Shutterstock Images, 19 (flag), 19 (peanuts), 19 (flower), 19 (peaches), 22–23, 24, 45; Ancha Chiangmai/Shutterstock Images, 19 (bird); Benjamin Albiach Galan/Shutterstock Images, 28–29; Jack Hong/Shutterstock Images, 30–31; Grindstone Media Group/Shutterstock Images, 33; Rob Wilson/Shutterstock Images, 35; Jack Thornell/AP/Shutterstock Images, 36–37

Editor: Marie Pearson
Series Designer: Joshua Olson

Library of Congress Control Number: 2021951401

Publisher's Cataloging-in-Publication Data

Names: Lawler, Margaret, author.
Title: Georgia / by Margaret Lawler
Description: Minneapolis, Minnesota : Abdo Publishing, 2023 | Series: Core library of US states | Includes online resources and index.
Identifiers: ISBN 9781532197512 (lib. bdg.) | ISBN 9781098270278 (ebook)
Subjects: LCSH: U.S. states--Juvenile literature. | Southeastern States--Juvenile literature. | Georgia--History--Juvenile literature. | Physical geography--United States--Juvenile literature.
Classification: DDC 975.8--dc23

Population demographics broken down by race and ethnicity come from the 2019 census estimate. Population totals come from the 2020 census.

CONTENTS

CHAPTER ONE

THE PEACH STATE

The peach trees in Georgia's Peach County are covered with fruit ready for harvest. It's early June. The county's annual Peach Festival is in full swing. Crowds of people gather to watch a parade. Vendors sell arts and crafts by the side of a road. The smell of sugary peaches fills the air. Chefs bring out the World's Largest Peach Cobbler, a dessert that they bake each year. It measures 5 feet by 11 feet (1.5 m by 3.4 m).

Peaches are an important part of Georgia's history and culture. People first

Peaches are one of many crops grown in Georgia.

MAP OF GEORGIA

Georgia has many places to explore. How does this map help you understand all that Georgia has to offer?

planted peaches in the region in the 1700s. Agriculture is still an important industry in Georgia. The state ranks third in the nation in peach production.

EXPLORING GEORGIA

Georgia is part of the US region called the South. The South is known for its warm weather and hospitality. Alabama borders Georgia to the west. Tennessee is to the north. South Carolina and the

PERSPECTIVES

ATLANTA'S GREEN SPACES

Atlanta is one of the fastest-growing cities in the United States. Between 2010 and 2019, more than 730,000 people became residents of the Atlanta metropolitan area. Many large cities, including Atlanta, have few parks or other green spaces. Natural spaces have positive impacts on mental health. Michael Halicki is the executive director of Park Pride, an Atlanta organization that works to create neighborhood parks. From 1989 to 2021, it helped promote the development of more than 250 parks. Describing undeveloped land in the city, Halicki says, "Those areas are now getting a second look as . . . places for contemplation and reflection."

Atlantic Ocean are to the east. And Florida runs along the southern border.

Georgia's state government has three branches. The legislative branch is called the General Assembly. It is made up of two sections, the Senate and House of Representatives. Each section has elected officials who create and vote on new bills. The governor leads the executive branch. The governor can sign bills into law. The third branch is the judicial branch. It is made up of the courts. The state's Supreme Court is the highest level of state court.

The state has several large cities.

UNIVERSITY OF GEORGIA

The University of Georgia (UGA) is Georgia's largest university. It opened in Athens, Georgia, in 1801. The city was named after the Greek city of Athens. The Greek city was historically a center of learning. Many famous Greek thinkers came from this city. UGA was the first state-chartered university in the United States. This means the school was founded by the state government.

Atlanta has several places to cool off in hot weather.

Atlanta is the biggest. It is also the state capital. The city has several museums and cultural centers. It is home to major sports teams such as the Braves baseball team and Falcons football team. Many large companies have headquarters in the city. They include Coca-Cola and the Home Depot.

Savannah is the oldest city in Georgia. It was founded in 1733. Today the city is a bustling mix of old and new. Savannah has one of the busiest ports on the East Coast. Some of its town squares are named after people from history. Greene Square honors Major-General Nathanael Greene of the Revolutionary War (1775–1783). He helped coordinate the fight against the British in Savannah.

Visitors to Georgia have many things to see and do outside of the cities. Mountains in the north give way to flatlands in the south. Warm weather allows farmers to grow many types of crops, including the state's famous peaches. Boaters and fishers enjoy freshwater lakes and rivers. People can watch sea turtles hatch on several of Georgia's islands. Many wealthy people make their homes on the state's islands too. Whether in the city or out in the country, Georgia has something for everyone.

STRAIGHT TO THE SOURCE

In 2020 Ashley Scott and Renee Walters bought land in Wilkinson County, Georgia. Their goal was to build a city where Black people would not face racism. Scott said:

> *One of the reasons we selected Wilkinson County is that from the first day, when we [visited the county], we never felt like we were unwelcome. . . . In Wilkinson County, people look at you like a human being, with dignity. They are creating an environment for success. . . .*
>
> *So that's where we are, being more intentional about the type of communities Black families need, . . . so that we can empower our children and the next generation of children to have a sense of pride and a sense of collective power to make change.*

Source: Ashley Scott. "We're Creating a City in Georgia for Black People to Live without Racism." *Newsweek*, 1 Nov. 2020, newsweek.com. Accessed 27 May 2021.

CONSIDER YOUR AUDIENCE

Adapt this passage for a different audience, such as your friends. Write a blog post conveying this same information for the new audience. How does your post differ from the original text and why?

HISTORY OF GEORGIA

People have lived in Georgia for approximately 12,000 years. The early peoples are known as Paleo-Indians. They made stone tools, such as spearheads and knives. The Paleo-Indians were hunters and gatherers. They traveled in small groups in search of food.

Over time, people began living in more permanent settlements. They started planting corn. They traded goods with nearby communities. A period of time called the Mississippian Period lasted from 800 CE to

Between 1000 and 1550 CE, thousands of American Indians lived at what is now Etowah Mounds State Historic Site.

1600 CE. During this time, people built more elaborate towns. They had houses with thatched roofs. Peoples of the Mississippian Culture built burial and ritual mounds. Some mounds can still be seen today at the Etowah Mounds State Historic Site in northwestern Georgia. Modern American Indian people, including the Muskogee (Creek) and Cherokee, can trace their histories back to peoples of the Mississippian Period.

COLONIAL HISTORY

Spanish explorers first arrived in the Georgia region in 1526. Some looked for gold and silver. Sometimes the explorers hurt and threatened American Indian people to try to learn where these metals were located. In addition, the explorers killed and enslaved American Indian people. Some Spanish explorers tried to convert these people to Christianity. The interactions between American Indians and Europeans exposed American Indians to new diseases. Many American Indians died from European diseases. Later interactions with English settlers also caused illnesses.

James Oglethorpe was from London, England.

In 1733 James Oglethorpe claimed Georgia as a colony of the British Empire. It became the thirteenth American colony. He and a group of other English colonists founded the town of Savannah. Georgia was the only American colony to be ruled by the Board of Trustees, which was located in London, England. The Board of Trustees banned slavery in Georgia, making it the only American colony where the practice was not allowed. But the colonists wanted to use slave labor to grow more crops. As the board's power weakened, the colony legalized slavery in 1751.

After slavery was legalized, many planters from nearby colonies flooded into Georgia with enslaved people. Georgia joined the African slave trade in 1765. Black Africans were enslaved and brought to the American colonies. Many worked on large farms called plantations. These farms became dependent on slave labor. Between 1750 and 1775, Georgia's enslaved population grew from fewer than 500 to more than 18,000. In some parts of Georgia, enslaved people outnumbered white people.

STATEHOOD AND BEYOND

By the 1760s tensions were rising between the American colonies and the British Empire. Georgia and the other colonies fought for independence from the British Empire during the Revolutionary War. The colonies won the war and gained independence.

After the war, the former colonists needed to create a new government. The new structure and laws were described in the US Constitution. The former colonies joined the new nation as states. Georgia became the fourth US state on January 2, 1788.

After Georgia's statehood, its growing population led to more conflicts with American Indians, often over land. President Andrew Jackson signed the Indian Removal Act in 1830. The US government forced American Indians in the southeast to exchange their homelands for land west of the Mississippi River. Many nations, including the Cherokee Nation, moved to Oklahoma. The journey to Oklahoma became known as the Trail of Tears. Thousands of American Indian people died.

PERSPECTIVES

JOHN ROSS

John Ross became the leader of the Cherokee Nation in 1827. He tried to convince US government officials to let the Cherokee Nation stay in Georgia. The US government wrote a treaty. Against Ross's wishes, some members of the Cherokee Nation accepted this treaty. They exchanged their land in Georgia for land in the West. Many Cherokee people were angry. Ross led efforts to rebuild once the nation arrived in its new territory.

Other conflicts were growing in

Georgia in the mid-1800s. Northern states thought slavery should be illegal. The economies of Georgia and other Southern states depended on slave labor to grow crops such as cotton. Georgia left the United States in 1861. It joined other Southern states to create the Confederacy. The remaining states were called the Union. The Confederacy and the Union fought in the American Civil War (1861–1865). The Union won the war. The Confederate states rejoined the United States. Slavery became illegal in the country.

Formerly enslaved people became citizens after the war. Black men were allowed to vote. Women were not allowed to vote at that time. However, Black Americans and other people of color were still not treated equally. In Georgia, white people made laws to keep people of color from voting. For example, some places required people to pay money to vote. Many people of color were unable to pay this fee. Other laws kept public spaces like schools and buses segregated. Some private

GEORGIA

QUICK FACTS

Georgia is unique from other states in many ways. Based on the chapter, why do you think people chose some of these state symbols?

Abbreviation: GA
Nickname: The Peach State
Motto: Wisdom, justice, and moderation
Date of statehood: January 2, 1788
Capital: Atlanta
Population: 10,711,908
Area: 59,425 square miles (153,910 sq km)

STATE SYMBOLS

State bird
Brown thrasher

State flower
Cherokee rose

State crop
Peanut

State fruit
Peach

ALBANY MOVEMENT

A major civil rights movement began in Albany, Georgia, in November 1961. It was known as the Albany Movement. It aimed to get rid of segregation in the community. Black students and other community members held nonviolent demonstrations. Their work attracted the attention of Martin Luther King Jr., a leader in the struggle for civil rights. Less than a month into the movement, police had put more than 500 protestors in jail. The movement was unsuccessful, and demonstrations ended in August 1962. But the efforts helped King organize other nonviolent protests in the South.

businesses also had a separate section for people of color.

In Georgia, people of color worked together to gain equal rights. The Savannah Men's Club formed in 1905. Black activists led the organization. They published their own newspaper, the *Savannah Tribune*. The group also held demonstrations for equal treatment. After many Black men returned from fighting for the United States in World War II, the sting of unequal treatment felt even greater. Black Georgian veterans and voters were especially emboldened. In 1946 it took just two months for more than 14,000 Black Georgians to register to vote. The struggle for civil rights reached its height in the 1960s. The Civil Rights Act of 1964 banned unfair treatment based on race, sex, or other characteristics. The struggle for equal treatment continues today.

EXPLORE ONLINE

Chapter Two discusses the struggle for racial equality in Georgia. The website below describes the civil rights movement in more detail. What information does the website give about the treatment of Black people in the United States? How is the information from the website similar to the information in Chapter Two? What new information did you learn?

CIVIL RIGHTS MOVEMENT

abdocorelibrary.com/georgia

CHAPTER THREE

GEOGRAPHY AND CLIMATE

Georgia has a wide range of geographic landscapes. The Appalachian Mountains extend into northwestern Georgia. Part of the Appalachian Mountains, the Blue Ridge Mountains, are in the northeast. These are the tallest mountains in the state. Brasstown Bald, the highest point in Georgia, is located in these mountains. It is 4,784 feet (1,458 m) above sea level. Lake Lanier, a popular tourist destination, is also in the Blue Ridge Mountains.

Some people enjoy visiting the Blue Ridge Mountains.

Boardwalks in Okefenokee Swamp allow visitors to explore without damaging the landscape.

Farther south, the land transitions into an area known as the Piedmont. The word *piedmont* means "foothill." The Piedmont is located in the foothills of the Appalachian Mountains. The area has low hills and shallow valleys.

The Coastal Plain is the southernmost region of the state. Most of Georgia's crops are grown there. But the

Coastal Plain also has longleaf pine forests, marshes, and swamps. The Okefenokee Swamp is in this region. It is the nation's largest freshwater swamp.

Georgia is rich in freshwater sources, with 70,150 miles (112,895 km) of rivers and streams. Major rivers include the Chattahoochee River and Oconee River. Some rivers, such as the Altamaha River, empty into the Atlantic Ocean.

PERSPECTIVES

CUMBERLAND ISLAND

Cumberland Island is Georgia's southernmost barrier island. Barrier islands form near the shore when waves and wind move rocks and sand. The National Park Service protects much of Cumberland Island. The island is full of wildlife, including armadillos and owls. Feral horses also roam there. Doug Hoffman is a biologist who works on the island. He often hears visitors comment about its natural beauty. "They don't hear the typical day to day hustle and bustle that they hear when they're in civilization," Hoffman says. "When they get here, all they hear is the birds singing or the wind blowing."

Georgia's climate varies with the region. But in general, the state experiences four seasons and warm temperatures. In winter, temperatures average above 40 degrees Fahrenheit (4°C). The state also receives a lot of rainfall. It averages between 50 and 60 inches (127 and 152 cm) each year. More rain falls in the northern mountains than in other parts of the state.

Some of the state's precipitation comes in the form of storms. Thunderstorms are more common in the summer. Georgia also experiences tropical storms and hurricanes. These are most likely to occur between June and November. Hurricanes form over warm ocean waters. When they reach land, they can cause damage from flooding and strong winds.

PLANTS AND ANIMALS

Georgia is home to many types of plants and animals. Some animals, such as the brown thrasher, are found throughout the state. The brown thrasher is

Georgia's state bird. The bird uses complex songs to communicate. It also imitates the songs of other birds.

Other plants and animals are more common in specific regions of Georgia. Maples, pines, and oaks grow in the forests of northern Georgia. These forests provide homes for many animals, including black bears, turkeys, and wild boars.

CHEROKEE ROSE

Georgia's state flower is the Cherokee rose. It's named after the Cherokee Nation, whose people grew the flower throughout the Southeast. The rose is also connected to the Trail of Tears. According to one legend, Cherokee elders prayed for protection during the long journey. The next morning, the roses bloomed where their tears had fallen. The Cherokee rose's thorny stems became a symbol of strength. The roses gave the Cherokee courage to begin their new nation.

Rivers and lakes across southern Georgia are full of life. Georgia's wetlands are home to 80 types of amphibians. These include bullfrogs and hellbenders, a type

Loggerhead sea turtles lay eggs on Georgia's beaches.

of salamander. Alligators live in freshwater swamps in the southern part of the state.

Georgia's coast is also home to unique animals. Loggerhead sea turtles return to the Atlantic coast each summer to lay eggs. Salt water and fresh water mix in the marshes along the coast. Grasses there attract many types of wildlife. Young crabs, oysters, and fish live in the marshes. They leave for the ocean when they are adults. More than 620 species of plants and 230 bird

species live in Okefenokee Swamp. There are many species of bats, frogs, salamanders, and more.

Some of the state's plants rely on Georgia's rainy weather. Georgia's state tree, the live oak, is one example. It grows faster and is healthier when it receives a lot of rain. The live oak can grow up to 80 feet (24 m) tall. Its large size creates wide areas of shade. The live oak can withstand strong hurricane winds.

CHAPTER FOUR

RESOURCES AND ECONOMY

Agriculture is Georgia's oldest industry. English colonists first grew crops such as cotton, indigo, and rice. Today nearly one in seven Georgia residents works in an agriculture or forestry-related job. Georgia is the top US producer of peanuts, blueberries, and spring onions.

Livestock is the largest part of Georgia's agricultural industry. Farmers raise chickens, cattle, goats, and even alligators.

Peanuts grow underground. Farmers dig them up and let them dry out before collecting the peanuts.

FILM AND MORE

Georgia is a major filming location for movies and television. Companies that film in the state can receive up to a 30 percent tax credit. A tax credit reduces the amount of taxes owed to the government. This tax credit also applies to other forms of entertainment, such as animation and video games. Georgia also has recording studios and the equipment needed to complete these projects. Several Marvel movies have been filmed in the state. Popular TV shows such as *Stranger Things* were also filmed in Georgia.

Many chicken farms are in the Piedmont area. However, the farming industry is present throughout the state.

Georgia has many natural resources. Approximately 60 percent of the land is forested. And the state has the most commercial forest land of any US state. It has one of the top forestry industries in the nation. Georgia is also the top US producer of clay and is famous for its high-quality marble. Georgia's marble was used in the statue of Abraham Lincoln at the Lincoln Memorial in Washington, DC.

Georgia's capitol building has stairs made of marble from the state.

MANUFACTURING

Georgia's manufacturing industry grew quickly in the 2000s. The industry was more than 10 percent of the state's economy in 2018. Some of Georgia's factories produce cars and airplanes. The state government

PERSPECTIVES

THE BUSIEST AIRPORT

For many years Hartsfield-Jackson Atlanta International Airport (ATL) was considered the busiest airport in the world. In 2019 more than 110 million passengers traveled through the airport. But beginning in late 2019, a disease called COVID-19 began spreading around the world. Many people stopped traveling to help slow the spread of the disease. As a result, ATL lost its title for 2020. Patrick Lucas is the vice president of economics for Airports Council International World. He said, "While the industry recovers, we expect ATL to retake its spot at the top in the coming years."

works with Georgia colleges and universities to make sure that manufacturing companies are run efficiently. This will help the industry last for years to come.

Atlanta houses the headquarters of several major companies. Coca-Cola was founded there in 1886. Today the company and the businesses that bottle its beverages employ more than 700,000 people worldwide. Delta Airlines is also based

The World of Coca-Cola Museum in Atlanta features the history of the company.

in Atlanta. It employs more than 33,000 people in Georgia. United Parcel Service (UPS) is another Atlanta-based company. The company delivers approximately 5.5 billion packages per year.

FURTHER EVIDENCE

Chapter Four covers Georgia's economy and resources. What is the main point of this chapter? What key evidence supports this point? Read the article at the website below. Does the information on the website support the main point of the chapter? Does it present new evidence?

AGRIBUSINESS

abdocorelibrary.com/georgia

EBENEZER

PEOPLE AND PLACES

Approximately 52 percent of Georgia's population is white people who are not Hispanic or Latino. And more than 30 percent of the population is Black. Many Georgia cities and towns were important locations for the civil rights movement in the mid-1900s. Today these cities honor the movement and its Black leaders. This is especially true in Atlanta, where historic churches and museums dot the city. They tell the story of that period in Georgia's history.

Ebenezer Baptist Church played a role in the civil rights movement. It also held Martin Luther King Jr.'s private funeral service.

Georgia also has a growing Latino population. Nearly 10 percent of the population is Hispanic or Latino. Young Latino voters have had a strong influence in political elections in recent years.

HISTORIC SAVANNAH

As the oldest city in Georgia, Savannah has many historic sites to enjoy. The oldest Black church in the country, First African Baptist Church, is located in Savannah. Historically the church was a safe place for enslaved people who had escaped. Elsewhere in the city, people can visit the birthplace of Juliette Gordon Low. In 1912 she founded Girl Scouts of the USA to inspire girls to be independent and adventurous. The Bonaventure Cemetery is another popular site for history and art lovers. The cemetery was built in the late 1700s and showcases the Southern Gothic art style.

Georgia was once home to many American Indians. Today less than 1 percent of the population is American Indian. There are no federally recognized tribes in Georgia. But the state recognizes three nations. They are the Cherokee of

Georgia, Georgia Tribe of Eastern Cherokee, and Lower Muskogee Creek Tribe.

Many famous people have come from Georgia. Rapper Montero Lamar Hill, better known as Lil Nas X, was born near Atlanta. Actress Chloë Grace Moretz is also from Atlanta. Civil rights activist Martin Luther King Jr. was born and grew up in Atlanta. President Jimmy Carter was born in Plains, Georgia. He worked on his parents' peanut farm before serving as US president from 1977 to 1981.

CITIES AND PLACES

Georgia is full of things to do and places to see. Visitors to Atlanta can tour Centennial Olympic Park, which Olympic athletes used during the 1996 Olympic Games. Today the park has fountains and walking paths. It is also close to the Georgia Aquarium and the College Football Hall of Fame.

For golf lovers, Augusta hosts the Masters Tournament. This is one of the major Professional

PERSPECTIVES

LEADING THE PEOPLE

John Lewis was a civil rights leader who worked alongside Martin Luther King Jr. and other activists. In the 1960s Lewis helped register Black voters in the South. Atlanta voters elected Lewis to the US House of Representatives in 1986. While in office, he worked to improve health care and education. He served in Congress until his death in 2020.

Golfers' Association (PGA) championships. Beautiful azaleas bloom during the tournament. Georgia native and golfer Bobby Jones cofounded the Masters Tournament.

Outside the cities and away from crowds, Georgia has even more to offer. Northern Georgia has several state parks. Some of these parks are inside the Chattahoochee-Oconee National Forest. Rivers, lakes, and hiking trails bring outdoor enthusiasts from around the country. Georgia's eventful history and beautiful landscapes provide many opportunities for visitors and locals alike.

STRAIGHT TO THE SOURCE

Kevin Langston worked for the Georgia Department of Economic Development. In a 2017 interview, he spoke of the sites Georgia has to offer:

> *We have new attractions, lodging, and restaurants opening all over the state, which should continue to draw tourists. The new stadiums in Atlanta have helped to draw some terrific, major events, including the College Football Championship Game. Up in North Georgia, we have exciting new zip lines. . . . In rural Georgia, agritourism is taking off, attracting people who want to know where their food originates, and enjoying some fantastic meals, close to the places where it is grown. I am very excited to see what the . . . future holds!*

Source: Parrish Walton. "Georgia's Tourism Industry Keeps 450,000 People Employed." *Georgia Public Broadcasting*, 12 June 2017, gpb.org. Accessed 12 May 2021.

BACK IT UP

The author of this passage is using evidence to support a point. Write a paragraph describing the point the author is making. Then write down two or three pieces of evidence the author uses to make the point.

IMPORTANT DATES

12,000 years ago

Paleo-Indians are the first people to live in the Georgia region.

1526

Spanish explorers first arrive in what is now Georgia.

1788

Georgia becomes the fourth US state on January 2.

1830

The US government passes the Indian Removal Act. The government forces many American Indians in Georgia to leave the state and move west.

1861–1865

Georgia fights for the Confederacy in the Civil War.

1961

The Albany Movement begins in Albany, Georgia. Black community members protest to end segregation.

1996
Atlanta hosts the Summer Olympic Games.

2010–2019
The Atlanta metropolitan area gains more than 730,000 new residents.

STOP AND THINK

Tell the Tale

Chapter One of this book describes the Georgia Peach Festival. Imagine you are attending this event. Write 200 words about your surroundings and what you are excited to do.

Dig Deeper

After reading this book, what questions do you still have about Georgia? With an adult's help, find a few reliable sources that can help you answer your questions. Write a paragraph about what you learned.

Another View

This book talks about Georgia's early history. As you know, every source is different. Ask a librarian or another adult to help you find another source about this topic. Write a short essay comparing and contrasting the new source's point of view with that of this book's author. What is the point of view of each author? How are they similar and why? How are they different and why?

Take a Stand

Many industries make up Georgia's economy. Some of these include agriculture, manufacturing, and entertainment. Which of these industries do you think is the most important, and why? How does this industry shape the state's identity?

activist
a person who takes action to make social or political changes

agritourism
a form of tourism that involves visiting farms and participating in agricultural activities

colony
an area of land that is separate from but controlled by another country

culture
the way a group of people lives; its customs, beliefs, and laws

feral
describing a domesticated animal that is living in the wild

hospitality
kind or generous treatment

manufacturing
the process of making items or parts for sale

metropolitan
describing an area that consists of a city or cities and their surrounding suburbs

precipitation
moisture in the form of rain or snow

ONLINE RESOURCES

To learn more about Georgia, visit our free resource websites below.

Visit **abdocorelibrary.com** or scan this QR code for free Common Core resources for teachers and students, including vetted activities, multimedia, and booklinks, for deeper subject comprehension.

Visit **abdobooklinks.com** or scan this QR code for free additional online weblinks for further learning. These links are routinely monitored and updated to provide the most current information available.

LEARN MORE

Harris, Duchess, and Tammy Gagne. *John Lewis.* Abdo, 2020.

Tekiela, Stan. *The Kids' Guide to Birds of Georgia.* Adventure Publications, 2020.

INDEX

About the Author

Margaret Lawler lives in Minnesota, where she edits and writes children's books. In her free time, she enjoys baking and playing board games.